God is Near

In health, in sickness,
In joy, in trouble...

God is Near

Bedside companion of Inspiration and Strength

Frank H. Crumpler

FLEMING H. REVELL COMPANY

Old Tappan, New Jersey

Library of Congress Cataloging in Publication Data

Crumpler, Frank H.
  God is near.

  1. Sick—Prayer books and devotions—English.
I. Title.
BV4910.C78   242'.4   73-1707
ISBN 0-8007-0589-0

TO
Glenda, Miriam, Mark, and Michael,
who are God's greatest gifts to me

Contents

Preface

This little book is designed to bring courage and faith to those who are in the difficult moments of life. In times of illness or confinement to the hospital bed, we need to know the nearness of God. His power is at work, and He is ready to bring comfort to you in your moment of need.

There are devotional readings to cover a period of twenty days. I suggest that you read *one* during each day of your illness. When you have read the selection for the day, try to memorize the verses on the preceding page. Let the spirit of God speak to your needs through each of these devotional messages. This can be your finest hour, even if you are ill. Keep asking God to use this time to help you become a better, stronger person.

Most illness brings the question, "Why did God allow this to happen?" That question might need to be left unanswered. Whatever the purpose God has for you, we know that His motive is one of *love*. ". . . God is love" (1 John 4:8). We can depend on that. May this series of messages meet a need in your life as day by day you walk with God, because He is near to you.

FRANK H. CRUMPLER

9

God is Near

ISAIAH 41:13

For I the Lord thy God will hold thy right hand,
saying unto thee, Fear not; I will help thee.

> For I, the Lord your God,
>   hold your right hand;
> it is I who say to you, "Fear not,
>   I will help you" (RSV).

I am holding you by your right hand—I, the Lord
your God—and I say to you, Don't be afraid; I
am here to help you (LB).

1
You Are Not Alone

For God has said, "I will never leave you; I will never abandon you." Let us be bold, then, and say, "The Lord is my helper, I will not be afraid. What can man do to me?"   HEBREWS 13:5,6 TE*

". . . and teach them to obey everything I have commanded you. And remember! I will be with you always, to the end of the age."
MATTHEW 28:20 TE*

And, behold, I am with thee, and will keep thee in all places whither thou goest, and will bring thee again into this land; for I will not leave thee until I have done that which I have spoken to thee of.   GENESIS 28:1.

Fear not, for I am with you, be not dismayed, for I am your God; I will strengthen you, I will help you, I will uphold you with my victorious right hand.   ISAIAH 41:10 RS*

Thou art near, O Lord; and all thy commandments are truth.   PSALMS 119:15

God is our refuge and strength, a very present help in trouble.   PSALMS 46:1 RS*

It is only natural for you to feel alone during illness or grief. Trouble seems to bring only confusion and loneliness into our lives. The feeling of being forsaken settles like a cloud upon our spirits. Yet, God's promises can brighten our spirits and cast out all our loneliness in a time of weakness. No matter how great your problems, you can cling to God's promises and find comfort in them today.

These verses remind us of God's presence. In each of them He is saying, "You are not alone, I am with you." Whatever your situation, He is right here to hold you up, regardless of your circumstances. He is there to make you adequate for any situation.

Accept this great fact today. God is by your side. Hold these promises close to your heart. Read them again and again. Tell yourself that these verses are directed to your heart and life. They were written for you. God is saying, "I am with you. You are not alone."

Spend a few moments in prayer, thanking God for His presence. Just say, "Thank you, Father, that I am not alone today. Thank you for being with me as I face these difficult circumstances." Then be very quiet and listen to Him as He says, "Fear not, for I am with you." He will strengthen you. He will help you. He will uphold you.

2
Fear Not

For I, the Lord your God, hold your right hand;
it is I who say to you, "Fear not, I will help you."
ISAIAH 41:13 RSV

"Come to me, all of you who are tired from car-
rying your heavy loads, and I will give you rest."
MATTHEW 11:28 TEV

Then Jesus said to them, "Why are you fright-
ened? Are you still without faith?"
MARK 4:40 TEV

Thou shalt not be afraid for the terror by night;
nor for the arrow that flieth by day; Nor for the
pestilence that walketh in darkness; nor for the
destruction that wasteth at noonday.
PSALMS 91:5,6

The Lord is my light and salvation; whom shall
I fear? The Lord is the stronghold of my life; of
whom shall I be afraid?
PSALMS 27:1 RSV

What time I am afraid, I will trust in thee.
PSALMS 56:3

Fear is one of the most tormenting emotions a person can experience. Almost everyone is afraid today. The fear of illness or death is common to us all. Some people fear growing old or the loss of physical or mental health. Many people are afraid of failure, while others are afraid of success. The future makes some of us afraid, while memories of the past frighten others. Sometimes we are just simply afraid to face ourselves or our circumstances.

The Bible has a lot to say about fear. Perhaps as you endure the pain and inconvenience of illness you are also haunted by the ghost of fear. We are also afraid of that which we do not understand. Fear can depress the spirits and keep us from the fullness of God's joy within.

Christ longs to set you free from your fears today. He wants you to bring your fears into the open—admit them, take a good long look at your fears. When you bring them out into the light you can understand them and conquer them more easily. Then turn your fears over to Christ. Since He is with you, all you have to do is recognize His presence and share with Him your problem. Remember that God is all-powerful. He can handle any problem you have. All you have to do is say to Him, "Father, I am afraid," and His power will move in to banish your fears. As you listen to His voice, you will hear Him say, "Be of good cheer; it is I; be not afraid" (Matthew 14:27).

3

Learn to Believe

Jesus said unto him, If thou canst believe, all things are possible to him that believeth.

MARK 9:23

Now faith is the substance of things hoped for, the evidence of things not seen. But without faith it is impossible to please him: for he that cometh to God must believe that he is, and that he is a rewarder of them that diligently seek him.

HEBREWS 11:1,6

And by him all that believe are justified from all things, from which ye could not be justified by the law of Moses.

ACTS 13:39

God condemned the cities of Sodom and Gomorrah, destroying them with fire, and made an example of them for the wicked, of what will happen to them.

2 PETER 2:6 TEV

And when he was come into the house, the blind men came to him: and Jesus saith unto them, Believe ye that I am able to do this? They said unto him, Yea, Lord.

MATTHEW 9:28

Faith is far more than belief. If a person is willing to accept as fact what he sees or has proved to him, that is belief. But, faith is that same willingness to accept as fact something that cannot be proven or seen. The writer of Hebrews described faith just that way. He said "Faith is . . . the evidence of things not seen" (Hebrews 11:1). We cannot prove that God exists, but faith does not require any proof. When a man believes in God, no proof is necessary, and when a man does not believe in God, no proof is good enough to convince him. The belief in God is all the evidence needed. Therefore, faith, toward God, is proof unto itself.

Augustine said, "Faith is to believe on the word of God, what we do not see, and its reward is to see and enjoy what we believe." God is seen only through the eyes of faith and He can be reached only by the hand of faith. Within every person there is the capacity to believe. When this capacity is directed toward God, it becomes faith which will grow into confidence if it is used. Jesus said to Thomas, who had doubted Him, ". . . because thou hast seen me, thou hast believed: blessed are they that have not seen, and yet have believed" (John 20:29). We cannot see love, but we do see its effect on people. We do not see God, but He has given each of us the ability to know Him and respond to Him and when we do, it is on the basis of faith. Our faith is the only response God will accept, and therefore we ought to say with the penitent man, "Lord, I believe; help thou mine unbelief" (Mark 9:24).

4

The Power of Prayer

"Ask, and you will receive; seek, and you will find; knock, and the door will be opened to you. For everyone who asks will receive, and he who seeks will find, and the door will be opened to him who knocks. Would any one of you fathers give his son a stone, when he asks for bread? Or would you give him a snake, when he asks you for fish? As bad as you are, you know how to give good things to your children. How much more, then, your Father in heaven will give good things to those who ask him!"   MATTHEW 7:7-11 TEV

"For this reason I tell you: When you pray and ask for something, believe that you have received it, and everything will be given you."

MARK 11:24 TEV

"And I will do whatever you ask for in my name, so that the Father's glory will be shown through the Son. If you ask me for anything in my name, I will do it."   JOHN 14:13,14 TEV

In the same way the Spirit also comes to help us, weak that we are. For we do not know how we ought to pray; the Spirit himself pleads with God for us, in groans that words cannot express.

ROMANS 8:26 TEV

Pray without ceasing.   1 THESSALONIANS 5:17

A great Christian of long ago said, "More things are wrought by prayer than this world dreams of." How true it is that prayer is the source of great power in our lives. Prayer is communion with God. It is a mistake to think of prayer only as speaking to God. We pray when we listen to Him, as well as when we speak.

God wants us to pray, to make known our desires and our needs. He wants us to speak to Him in an attitude of repentance—calling on Him to forgive us of our sins. God wants us to pray the prayer of confession as we admit to Him our weaknesses and failures. The Bible teaches us to pray continually; that is, always living in an attitude of prayer. Yet prayer must include listening to the Lord.

Perhaps this is a part of the reason for your illness. It is God's way of saying, "Slow down, be still and listen to me." Sometimes the Lord has to stop us, even put us flat on our backs in order to make us attentive to His voice. Christ taught His disciples to pray confidently. We should always ask Him for whatever we desire, giving careful attention to the words "Thy will be done." Prayer changes things and people. Prayer can change you. Why not take advantage of these moments of quietness and realize the power of prayer in your own life?

5

Help for a Troubled Heart

"Do not be worried and upset," Jesus told them. "Believe in God, and believe also in me. There are many rooms in my Father's house, and I am going to prepare a place for you. I would not tell you this if it were not so. And after I go and prepare a place for you, I will come back and take you to myself, so that you will be where I am. You know how to get to the place where I am going." Thomas said to him, "Lord, we do not know where you are going; how can we know the way to get there?" Jesus answered him: "I am the way, I am the truth, I am the life; no one goes to the Father except by me. JOHN 14:1-6 TEV

When the cares of my heart are many, thy consolations cheer my soul. PSALMS 94:19 RSV

For where your treasure is, there will your heart be also. LUKE 12:34

That Christ may dwell in your hearts by faith; that ye, being rooted and grounded in love, May be able to comprehend with all saints what is the breadth, and length, and depth, and height; And to know the love of Christ, which passeth knowledge, that ye might be filled with all the fulness of God. EPHESIANS 3:17-19

The troubles of my heart are enlarged: O bring thou me out of my distresses. Look upon mine affliction and my pain; and forgive all my sins.
PSALMS 25:17,18

Many of the burdens you are called upon to bear in life weigh heavily on the heart. The heart is the seat of your emotions, the very center of your feelings. Our Lord spoke to His disciples to comfort them and to lift their spirits. He began by saying "Let not your heart be troubled . . ." (John 14:1).

Hearts are troubled because of physical suffering and pain. Hearts are troubled by unpleasant circumstances in the lives of other people about us. There are defeats, afflictions, and disappointments that seem to crush in upon the heart. Yet, God is still saying "Let not your heart be troubled."

God does not willingly bring suffering and pain upon us. He assures us that He will bear every burden for us. Practice these simple suggestions today in order that your spirit might be lifted: First, believe that God is able to handle any situation. Secondly, tell Him that you are placing the burden of your heart into His hands, and finally, thank God for His help as if you had already received it. Remember that burdens are blessings when they bring us closer to Christ.

6
Win Over Worry

Trust in the Lord, and do good; so shalt thou dwell in the land, and verily thou shalt be fed. Delight thyself also in the Lord; and he shall give thee the desires of thine heart. Commit thy way unto the Lord; trust also in him; and he shall bring it to pass.   PSALMS 37:3-5

Strengthen ye the weak hands, and confirm the feeble knees. Say to them that are of a fearful heart, Be strong, fear not: behold, your God will come with vengeance, even God with a recompence; he will come and save you.   ISAIAH 35:3,4

Wherefore lift up the hands which hang down, and the feeble knees.   HEBREWS 12:12

Therefore I will look unto the Lord; I will wait for the God of my salvation: my God will hear me.
                                                 MICAH 7:7

. . . I cried by reason of mine affliction unto the Lord, and he heard me; out of the belly of hell cried I, and thou heardest my voice.   JONAH 2:2

Worry is like a child riding a rocking horse—it never gets you anywhere, but it certainly keeps you busy. It is good to remember that most of the things we worry about never happen. Worry and anxiety cannot change the future nor the past, yet both can ruin a perfectly good present. God wants to give you victory over worry. He has the power to sustain you at all times. He is Lord over the problems of your life.

The promises in these verses assure us that God will help you in your moment of need. He is awaiting to help you now if only you will let Him. There are five key words in Psalm 37 which will help you overcome worry if you will obey them.

1. "Trust in the Lord." Put your full confidence in Him. Tell Him you are placing all your faith in Him. Leave every worry in His hands.

2. "Delight yourself in the Lord." Remind yourself of all the good things God has done for you. Thank Him for all His many blessings to you.

3. "Commit thy way unto the Lord." Place all your circumstances in God's hands. Tell Him you are giving Him your past, present, and future. Make God the controlling force in your life now.

4. "Rest in the Lord." Put your mind and heart at rest by turning all your problems over to Him.

5. "Wait patiently for Him." Make up your mind that God will take care of you in His own time. It is important that you wait patiently for Him to act in your life. The answer is not far from you, but be willing to wait. God moves when *He* alone is ready.

7
Cure for Conflict

Love one another warmly as brothers in Christ, and be eager to show respect for one another.
ROMANS 12:10 TEV

A soft answer turns away wrath, but a harsh word stirs up anger.   PROVERBS 15:1 RSV

Be ye angry, and sin not: let not the sun go down upon your wrath.   EPHESIANS 4:26

Wherefore, my beloved brethren, let every man be swift to hear, slow to speak, slow to wrath.
JAMES 1:19

Anger and personal conflict are common to all of us. There are times when we are almost forced to fight back or to lash out at someone who has wronged us. Yet, a wise person knows that getting mad has only harmful effects upon himself and others about him. Also, anger and conflict with others makes the spirit depressed and destroys the sense of well-being which is necessary to good health. By trying to control your feelings of anger you will be amazed at how much self-control you can develop. Try these simple suggestions for today.

1. Think of the person you have had conflict with and spend a few minutes in prayer for that individual. Pray for him by name and pray sincerely. You will find that you can't dislike someone you pray for.

2. Ask God to take away the conflict and resentment which you feel for that person. God can remove the hostility.

3. Spend a few minutes today planning some way to show kindness and Christian love to the person who might have made you angry. That is the Christlike thing to do.

The next time you feel anger rising up in you, follow these three suggestions, and you will find the key to a happy relationship with the one with whom you have conflict.

8

God Our Protection

At all times carry faith as a shield; with it you will be able to put out all the burning arrows shot by the Evil One. And accept salvation for a helmet, and the word of God as the sword that the Spirit gives you.   EPHESIANS 6:16,17 TEV

For he shall give his angels charge over thee, to keep thee in all thy ways.   PSALMS 91:11

And my God, with all his abundant wealth in Christ Jesus, will supply all your needs.
                    PHILIPPIANS 4:19 TEV

God will take care of you, but He wants you to depend upon Him. It is not always easy to *trust* in God's protection. You need to work at it. Today is a gift from God. Live it as if you are grateful to Him for giving you another day of life. Now stop and recognize that God has promised to be a shield to you and keep you from harm. He will keep you up and defend you by His power. He will meet your needs and fill all the empty spots in your life. This He has promised.

Now that you are in the hospital or confined to the bed at home, you can put into practice this principle of faith. Today spend some time counting your blessings: the family, the friends, kindness shown you by others, the joys you have had, the many ways in which God has helped you when you needed Him. Dwell on these blessings and keep thanking God for what He is going to do for you. Place your full confidence in Him and just remember that He will never fail you. Keep counting those blessings.

9

God Cares for You

Our high priest is not one who cannot feel sympathy with our weaknesses. On the contrary, we have a high priest who was tempted in every way that we are, but did not sin. Let us be brave, then, and come forward to God's throne, where there is grace. There we will receive mercy and find grace to help us just when we need it.

HEBREWS 4:15,16 TEV

Humble yourselves, then, under God's mighty hand, so that he will lift you up in his own good time. Throw all your worries on him, for he cares for you. 1 PETER 5:6,7 TEV

That led them through the deep, as an horse in the wilderness, that they should not stumble?

ISAIAH 63:13

Our human feelings cause us to think we are forsaken or forgotten in a time of trouble. Yet, we must remember that God has promised never to leave you or forsake you. God never forgets us when trouble comes. Your illness gives you a unique opportunity to practice the presence of Christ.

Today, remember that God has all power and all wisdom. He knows your needs and the deep longings of your heart. He can and will rescue you from your darkest hour. There is no substitute for a heart full of faith. Just believe God's promise of *care* for you and your situation. Take time now to thank Him for His presence with you. Open your inner heart to Him and tell Him everything that concerns you. Now as you pray rely on His power and presence as never before. Keep thanking God for giving you strength to bear your infirmity. Thank Him for hearing and understanding the burdens of your heart and life. He is right there by your side and He will lift you up in His own good time. Depend on Him to do that.

10

Deliverance from Depression

A merry heart doeth good like a medicine: but a broken spirit drieth the bones.   PROVERBS 17:22

These things have I spoken unto you, that my joy might remain in you, and that your joy might be full.   JOHN 15:11

Nothwithstanding in this rejoice not, that the spirits are subject unto you; but rather rejoice, because your names are written in heaven.

LUKE 10:20

In my distress I cried unto the Lord, and he heard me.   PSALMS 120:1

Depression is said to be the low state of the emotions that goes along with a sense of personal loss. When our well-being and security are threatened, the spirits usually suffer. A broken spirit is the cause of much of the emotional, mental, and physical suffering in the world today. Perhaps the medicine you need at this moment is a merry heart. You can get up off your face and smile at the problems around you with God's help. Let me make a few suggestions that will help you do just that.

First, remember that there is nothing God cannot do. He is the Master of the impossible. His power is too great for your mind to take it in. Don't depend on your strength to conquer these difficulties. God's help is available to you.

Secondly, think of the ways in which God has blessed you already. Family, friends, faith, and His guidance in your life are just a few of the good things He has brought to you. Remind yourself of God's goodness to you.

Finally, use this time of crisis or difficulty as an opportunity to show your faith in God. He knows whom He can trust with this kind of problem. Your merry heart will show God to someone else. Let Him lift your spirits now.

MICAH 7:7

Therefore I will look unto the Lord; I will wait for the God of my salvation: my God will hear me.

> But as for me, I will look to the
>   Lord,
> I will wait for the God of my salvation;
>   my God will hear me (RSV).

As for me, I look to the Lord for his help; I wait for God to save me; he will hear me (LB).

11

Dealing With Discouragement

Comfort ye, comfort ye my people, saith your God. Speak ye comfortably to Jerusalem, and cry unto her, that her warfare is accomplished, that her iniquity is pardoned: for she hath received of the Lord's hand double for all her sins. The voice of him that crieth in the wilderness, prepare ye the way of the Lord, make straight in the desert a highway for our God. ISAIAH 40:1-3

Therefore I will look unto the Lord; I will wait for the God of my salvation: my God will hear me. MICAH 7:7

He is despised and rejected of men; a man of sorrows, and acquainted with grief: and we hid as it were, our faces from him; he was despised, and we esteemed him not. Surely he hath borne our griefs, and carried our sorrows: yet we did esteem him stricken, smitten of God, and afflicted. ISAIAH 53:3,4

Discouragement can clip the wings of the soul and sadden the spirit. But let's never forget that this enemy of happiness we call discouragement can be defeated. When life seems dark and meaningless, it is time to take a good look at it and ask what is wrong. Usually we see more of the bad than the good. When we become involved with discouragement, it is easy to forget the deliverance of God. He has never failed you and He will not fail you now. There are several weapons of the spirit that can be used to slay the dragon of discouragement.

The first is faith. Begin now to reassure yourself that God is at work in your life—yes, He is at work in this situation of your life. Spend some moments in prayer and tell God of your belief in Him. Ask Him to help you see His hand at work in your life. His purpose and plan for you can only be seen through the eyes of faith. Let yourself rest in this faith and express your faith to God in prayer. This can be a good day for you as you fellowship with God's Holy Spirit. He will banish the cloud of discouragement if only you will let Him.

12
Keep on Praying

Don't worry about anything, but in all your prayers ask God for what you need, always asking him with a thankful heart. And God's peace, which is far beyond human understanding, will keep your hearts and minds safe, in Christ Jesus.

PHILIPPIANS 4:6,7 TEV

Is any among you afflicted? let him pray. Is any merry? let him sing psalms. Is any sick among you? let him call for the elders of the church; and let them pray over him, anointing him with oil in the name of the Lord: And the prayer of faith shall save the sick, and the Lord shall raise him up; and if he have committed sins, they shall be forgiven him. JAMES 5:13-18

This is why we have courage in God's presence; we are sure that he will hear us if we ask him for anything that is according to his will. He hears us whenever we ask him; since we know this is true, we know also that he gives us what we ask from him. 1 JOHN 5:14 TEV

Use your imagination to picture Christ standing beside you at this moment. He places His hand on your shoulder and you can see directly into His face. He is listening to you and waiting for you to speak your heart to Him. Now with that fact in mind, you can have real communion with God in prayer. He reads the thoughts of your mind so you need not speak your prayers aloud. In silence and sincerity you can experience the release of all your anxiety and fear. God wants you to know the joy of unburdening your heart to Him in prayer. God can hear and answer all His children at once. As a parent I have discovered the futility of hearing or speaking to more than one child at a time. It is impossible for you or me, but not for God. He hears all of His children at once and He is never too busy to attend to our faintest prayer. Be sure that you do not let the problem you face keep you from spending those precious moments in prayer. Take time now to listen to God and to speak your heart desires to Him. He is waiting to hear your prayer.

13
Seek God's Will

Do not be like them; your Father already knows what you need before you ask him. This is the way you should pray: "Our Father in heaven: May your name be kept holy, May your Kingdom come, May your will be done on earth as it is in heaven. Give us today the food we need; Forgive us the wrongs that we have done, As we forgive the wrongs that others have done us; Do not bring us to hard testing, but keep us safe from the Evil One." MATTHEW 6:8-13 TEV

Instead, give first place to his Kingdom and to what he requires, and he will provide you with all these other things. MATTHEW 6:33 TEV

And ye shall seek me, and find me, when ye shall search for me with all your heart.
JEREMIAH 29:13

And I tell you, Ask, and it will be given you; seek, and you will find; knock, and it will be opened to you. For every one who asks receives, and he who seeks finds, and to him who knocks it will be opened. LUKE 11:9,10 RSV

Finding the will of God begins with desire. To *want* God's will to be done in your life is the best place to start. When you become caught up with a desire to be and to do all God wants of you, that is an indication you are on the right track. God has a purpose for your life. There is a reason behind everything that happens to you. Perhaps even the problems and burdens are to refine the golden qualities within you.

The garden of Gethsemane was the site of the greatest battle this world has ever known. Our Lord fought there with all the forces of evil and He was victorious. Christ won when He uttered these words to the Father: ". . . nevertheless not my will, but thine, be done" (Luke 22:42). There is nothing that will invoke God's presence and power into your life any more certainly than those words. God wants to bring His will into focus in you. If you desire His will and seek His will, you will find it— that is His promise to you. Ask God to make His will perfected in you. Surrender to His purpose and the knowledge of His will follows close behind.

14
Escape from Temptation

Every temptation that has come your way is the kind that normally comes to people. For God keeps his promise, and he will not allow you to be tempted beyond your power to resist; but at the time you are tempted he will give you the strength to endure it, and so provide you with a way out.

1 CORINTHIANS 10:13 TEV

For I reckon that the sufferings of this present time are not worthy to be compared with the glory which shall be revealed in us.   ROMANS 8:18

Who shall separate us from the love of Christ? shall tribulation, or distress, or persecution, or famine, or nakedness, or peril, or sword? As it is written, For thy sake we are killed all the day long; we are accounted as sheep for the slaughter. Nay, in all these things we are more than conquerors through him that loved us. For I am persuaded, that neither death, nor life, nor angels, nor principalities, nor powers, nor things present, nor things to come, Nor height, nor depth, nor any other creature, shall be able to separate us from the love of God, which is in Christ Jesus our Lord.

ROMANS 8:35-39

These passages tell us how to meet and overcome temptation. Actually, there is no magic formula for dealing with the unholy desires of our lives, but there are some guidelines which I want to mention. First, you need to develop a strong desire to overcome the failures and shortcomings of your life. Usually we do whatever we strongly want to do. Be honest with yourself. Strive to change your desires from the things that would keep you from being your best self. Ask God to help you change your desires to the point that you really want to overcome temptation. Every moment of resistance to sin is a victory. After you begin to desire victory, remove yourself from harm's way. Keep yourself out of sin's path and get as far from the temptation as you can. This is a way to put your desire into practice. If we keep ourselves from opportunities, God will keep us from sin. As you practice the presence of God in your daily life, you will rely more on His strength. In His power there is victory. Remember that His strength is made perfect in your weakness. Spend time today thanking God for the power to overcome temptation. He is near.

15

His Grace Is Sufficient

His answer was, "My grace is all you need; for my power is strongest when you are weak." I am most happy, then, to be proud of my weaknesses, in order to feel the protection of Christ's power over me.   2 CORINTHIANS 12:9 TEV

May our Lord Jesus Christ himself, and God our Father, who loved us and in his grace gave us eternal courage and a good hope, fill your hearts with courage and make you strong to do and say all that is good.   2 THESSALONIANS 2:16, 17 TEV

From the end of the earth will I cry unto thee, when my heart is overwhelmed: lead me to the rock that is higher than I.   PSALMS 61:2

These verses fall on your heart like raindrops on a dry, parched desert. Here is manna for our wilderness. God's promise is to you. He will see you through every trial. Henry Ward Beecher said, "We are always in the forge or on the anvil; by trials God is shaping us for higher things." Beecher was right. Trials and heartaches are common to us all. You need to know the assurance of God's sustaining grace. What is grace? It is God's favor and goodness to us when we do not deserve it. Remember that we never deserve the blessings God showers upon us. God's grace is the quality that holds us up in the face of trouble and sorrow—sustaining grace. Now comfort your heart with these promises of God. Read the verses on the previous page slowly and meditate on them. Try to commit them to memory so you can say them with your eyes closed. In your mind's eye see yourself as standing on the mighty rock of God's grace so that nothing can disturb you. Hold on to His hand and let Him hold you up today.

16

Our Hope Is in the Lord

Why are you cast down, O my soul, and why are you disquieted within me? Hope in God; for I shall again praise him, my help and my God.

PSALMS 42:5,6 RSV

For it was by hope that we were saved; but if we see what we hope for, then it is not really hope. For who hopes for something that he sees?

ROMANS 8:24 TEV

We have this hope as an anchor for our hearts. It is safe and sure, and goes through the curtain of the heavenly temple into the inner sanctuary.

HEBREWS 6:19 TEV

Meanwhile these three remain: faith, hope, and love; and the greatest of these is love.

1 CORINTHIANS 13:13 TEV

Hope is the most beneficial of all the affections, and does much to prolong and strengthen life. Hope is the chief blessing of the spirit of man and our best possession. Before you give up hope, turn back and read these verses for today. In Psalm 42 we are reminded to hope in God when we are "cast down" or when we are "disquieted." Perhaps today you have reached the point of despair and complete dejection. If so, you should remember that nothing is beyond the scope of God's power. He is the God of the impossible who makes victory of what seems to be defeat. Hope rescues us from all the frustrations of life. During every crisis of life, even *this* crisis, you can cling to this genuine hope in God. Hope is the quality of soul and mind that helps you to see the brighter side of your circumstances. Hope sees a solution, a way out. Hope sees difficulty as an answer to the unanswered questions of the heart. Let God become very real to you now as you place all your confidence in Him. Fix your mind and heart on the hope you have in God.

17

God Hears Our Prayers

"And I will do whatever you ask for in my name, so that the Father's glory will be shown through the Son. If you ask me for anything in my name, I will do it."   JOHN 14:13,14 TEV

Thou hast heard my voice: hide not thine ear at my breathing, at my cry. Thou drewest near in the day that I called upon thee: thou saidst, Fear not.   LAMENTATIONS 3:56,57

As for me, I will call upon God; and the Lord shall save me.   PSALMS 55:16

I am as one mocked of his neighbour, who calleth upon God, and he answereth him: the just upright man is laughed to scorn.   JOB 12:4

Our God is the God of answered prayer. He hears the cries of our hearts whenever that cry goes out. St. Ambrose of Milan said, "Prayer is the wing wherewith the soul flies to heaven . . ." God hears and answers prayer. His ear is always attentive to the slightest prayer of His children. He wants us to pray. The very act of prayer, communion with God, gives to God the honor and glory due to His name. Words do not matter. Eloquence of speech is not the measure of effective prayer. In fact, the most sincere prayer is often spoken in the silence of the inner heart. God hears us even when we do not put our prayers into words. His spirit takes the deep feelings of the heart and translates them as prayer before the Father. As Thomas Brooks reminds us, "God hears no more than the heart speaks; and if the heart be dumb, God will certainly be deaf." Yet, you can be sure that when the heart speaks out, God always hears it. Will you stop right this moment to pray silently? Ask God to give you the assurance that He is near and that He hears your prayer. Place your burden at His feet today as you pray. Be bold before Him for He hears and will answer your prayer.

18

God Is Our Refuge

God is our refuge and strength, a very present help in trouble. Therefore will not we fear, though the earth be removed, and though the mountains be carried into the midst of the sea; Though the waters thereof roar and be troubled, though the mountains shake with the swelling thereof. Selah. There is a river, the streams whereof shall make glad the city of God, the holy place of the tabernacles of the most High. God is in the midst of her; she shall not be moved: God shall help her, and that right early. The heathen raged, the kingdoms were moved: he uttered his voice, the earth melted. The Lord of hosts is with us; the God of Jacob is our refuge. Selah. Come, behold the works of the Lord, what desolations he hath made in the earth. PSALMS 46:1-8

This is a most important promise which God makes to us. He is our refuge and strength. No matter how awesome your problems, you need have no fear. Certainly there are times when the spirits are low and you are weak. Yet, let the verses from Psalm 46 bring comfort to you today. God says He will strengthen you. In fact, He will be the mighty fortress and foundation beneath you. His power can make you adequate for any situation.

Almost daily we need to be aware that our personal problems can be solved by the guidance of our Heavenly Father. God wants us to depend upon Him for protection and deliverance. Even if the elements reverse their natural order or the courses of nature are disrupted, we can abide in God in peace. Find time today to put yourself at rest in this assurance of God's strength. Keep your mind on the fact of His nearness to you. Place the difficulties of your life in His hands at this moment. In quietness and confidence you can find the way to happiness and blessings. Let Him become your refuge today and He will restore you. Let Him give you new power over difficulties and transform your soul with His strength.

19

The Greatness of God

Great is the Lord, and greatly to be praised; and his greatness is unsearchable. One generation shall praise thy works to another, and shall declare thy mighty acts. PSALMS 145:3,4

Why boastest thou thyself in mischief, O mighty man? The goodness of God endureth continually. PSALMS 52:1

The Lord is good unto them that wait for him, to the soul that seeketh him. LAMENTATIONS 3:25

He loveth righteousness and judgment: the earth is full of the goodness of the Lord. PSALMS 33:5

Here is a fact we must never forget—God is good. His goodness is available to you in this hour. The passage on the preceding page assures us that God is gracious, full of compassion, and great in mercy. The Lord is good to all. At times we do not recognize His acts as good, but everything God does in or to our lives is from a motive of love. You can find deliverance from the sorrow and pain you experience today if you will follow these simple steps.

1. Conceive of the greatness and goodness of God. Imagine yourself in the palm of His hand. He has control of your life as you yield yourself to Him.

2. Speak to someone today about God's goodness to you. Let God's grace to you be known to someone else. The expression of your blessings will help you and the person who hears of them.

3. Thank God from deep within your heart for the benefits He has given to you. Count your blessings today and be grateful to Him for each one of them.

20
The Great Physician

And everywhere Jesus went, to villages, towns, or farms, people would take their sick to the market places and beg him to let the sick at least touch the edge of his cloak; and all who touched it were made well.   MARK 6:56 TEV

Who forgiveth all thine iniquities; who healeth all thy diseases.   PSALMS 103:3

The Lord also will be a refuge for the oppressed, a refuge in times of trouble.   PSALMS 9:9

Christ is still the Great Physician. He can heal the body, mind, and spirit today as in the days of His earthly life. God wants to take a vital part in your troubles today—the physical as well as the spiritual. No pain, nor hardship, nor opposition, nor even death itself can really harm you for God is with you. His skill exceeds that of any earthly physician. His wisdom surrounds you and every circumstance of your life. You can rest in the confidence that the Great Physician is attending you.

Jesus Christ is able to heal the personality by bringing you into completeness. To experience His healing power is to simply, sincerely want Him to touch you. Yield yourself to Him willingly. You must make the first move, however timidly it may be. He will respond with the miraculous touch that makes you whole in body, mind, and soul. Meditate upon these verses and they will endow you with deep serenity. Ask God to be the Great Physician to you in your need. Trust Him to bring healing and comfort to you today. Believe that He is at work in your life today and receive the healing He offers you.

LAMENTATIONS 3:25

The Lord is good unto them that wait for him, to the soul that seeketh him.

> The Lord is good to those who wait
>   for him,
> to the soul that seeks him (RSV).

The Lord is wonderfully good to those who wait for him, to those who seek for him (LB).

Index
of
Scripture References

NEW TESTAMENT

Matthew	6:8-13	40
	6:33	40
	7:7-11	20
	9:28	18
	11:28	16
	28:20	14
Mark	4:40	16
	6:56	54
	9:23	18
	11:24	20
Luke	10:20	32
	11:9,10	40
	12:34	22
John	14:1-6	22
	14:13,14	20, 48
	15:11	32
Acts	13:39	18
Romans	8:18	42
	8:24	46
	8:26	20
	8:35-39	42
	12:10	26
1 Corinthians	10:13	42
	13:13	46

OLD TESTAMENT